The Little Painter

PHASE 5
/er/ou/

Level 8 – Purple

BookLife Readers

Helpful Hints for Reading at Home

The graphemes (written letters) and phonemes (units of sound) used throughout this series are aligned with Letters and Sounds. This offers a consistent approach to learning, whether reading at home or in the classroom.

HERE IS A LIST OF PHONEMES FOR THIS PHASE OF LEARNING. AN EXAMPLE OF THE PRONUNCIATION CAN BE FOUND IN BRACKETS.

Phase 5			
ay (day)	ou (out)	ie (tie)	ea (eat)
oy (boy)	ir (girl)	ue (blue)	aw (saw)
wh (when)	ph (photo)	ew (new)	oe (toe)
au (Paul)	a_e (make)	e_e (these)	i_e (like)
o_e (home)	u_e (rule)		

Phase 5 Alternative Pronunciations of Graphemes			
a (hat, what)	e (bed, she)	i (fin, find)	o (hot, so, other)
u (but, unit)	c (cat, cent)	g (got, giant)	ow (cow, blow)
ie (tied, field)	ea (eat, bread)	er (farmer, herb)	ch (chin, school, chef)
y (yes, by, very)	ou (out, shoulder, could, you)		

HERE ARE SOME WORDS WHICH YOUR CHILD MAY FIND TRICKY.

Phase 5 Tricky Words			
oh	their	people	Mr
Mrs	looked	called	asked
could			

TOP TIPS FOR HELPING YOUR CHILD TO READ:

- Allow children time to break down unfamiliar words into units of sound and then encourage children to string these sounds together to create the word.

- Encourage your child to point out any focus phonics when they are used.

- Read through the book more than once to grow confidence.

- Ask simple questions about the text to assess understanding.

- Encourage children to use illustrations as prompts.

PHASE 5 /er/ou/

This book focuses on /er/ and /ou/ and the alternative pronunciations of its grapheme. It is a Purple level 8 book band.

The Little Painter

Written by
Shalini Vallepur

Illustrated by
Irene Renon

"Fernanda, are you awake?" Mama whispered.
"Hmph..." said Fernanda.
It was time for carnival. But Fernanda was not outside dancing with her friends in the dance troupe. She was cooped up in bed with an illness instead.

"How are you feeling? You look much better," said Mama. "Would you like some hot soup for when you watch the carnival?"

"Dancing is in my soul, Mama. I would prefer to dance in the carnival, not watch it from here," Fernanda said, pulling the curtains open.

"You are full of germs," said Mama. "Besides, look what I bought today. It's a paint set."
"I'm a dancer, not a painter. I'm rubbish at painting." Fernanda hunched her shoulders.
"That's because you worry about painting in a perfect way," said Mama.

"What should I paint, then?" Fernanda asked. "Whatever you like. You could paint your fern," said Mama.

"This is canvas. It's something you can paint on," said Mama. She found lots of paintbrushes and got Fernanda a pot of water. Just then, somebody shouted from outside.

Fernanda rushed to the window. Her friends Ana, Lucas and Lou were outside.
"Fernanda! Fernanda!" called Lou. "Look at my wonderful costume!" Lou twirled round and round.

"Are you better?" Ana asked. "Please come to the carnival."
Just then, a troupe of dancers came past. "We have to go. We miss you, Fernanda," said Lucas. "See you later!"

The carnival began. Fernanda heard the trumpets tooting and drums booming. People who were not dancing enjoyed the music from the kerb. Fernanda wanted to dance in the troupe with her friends.

"Why don't you give painting a go?" Mama said, handing Fernanda a paintbrush. "Make a start on that fern."

Fernanda took a closer look at the fern. She could see shades of dark green and bits of light green on the leaves. She moved the fern into the light and could see shiny bits of yellow.

With a swish here and a flick there, Fernanda began to paint the fern.

"What do you think, Mama?" said Fernanda, holding the finished fern painting.
"That is fantastic, Fernanda!" said Mama.

"I'm going to put it up in the kitchen," said Mama.
"It's not perfect..." Fernanda said.
"It does not have to be," Mama smiled.

Fernanda was ready to paint again the next morning.
"I want to paint something different today. I could paint a person," said Fernanda.

"If you feel better, you could paint the carnival," said Mama.

"That is a super idea, Mama!" said Fernanda, jumping up from the table.

Fernanda gave it her best shot. She perched on a stool and tried to paint the feathery headdresses and glittery costumes. It was not going well.

She could not focus. The dancers were twirling, spinning and moving around so fast that it was too difficult to paint them.

"How is your painting of the carnival?" Mama asked.

"It's terrible! It would be a lot easier if the dancers were standing still," said Fernanda. "I give up."

Knock! Knock! Knock!

"Someone is here," said Mama, rushing to answer it.

"Can they help with my painting?" Fernanda moaned.

Fernanda's friends had come to see her.
"We brought you some cake to get better," said Lou.
"And some flowers from the carnival to perk you up," said Lucas.

"The troupe missed having its best dancer," said Ana. "We hope you weren't too bored." "Thank you for visiting me!" said Fernanda. "I have been painting."

"I've got an idea... You three can pose for me!" said Fernanda. "The carnival outside moves too fast. If you stand still, I can paint your costumes and get it right."

The three friends were happy to pose for Fernanda's painting. They stood very still while Fernanda carried on with her painting.

"That looks perfect!" said Lou.
"I could add more paint to the shoulders..." said Fernanda.
"No, I think it's great the way it is," said Ana.

"Look at you! Our little painter," said Lucas. "Next year you could paint the carnival instead of dancing in it!"

"I think I will do both!" said Fernanda.

The Little Painter

1. Why couldn't Fernanda dance in the dance troupe?

2. What was the first thing that Fernanda painted?
   (a) A fern
   (b) A book
   (c) A doll

3. Why couldn't Fernanda paint the carnival?

4. What did Fernanda's friends bring her to make her feel better?

5. Fernanda thought that she was bad at painting, but she was very good. What kind of things are you good at? Is there anything new that you want to try?

BookLife PUBLISHING

BookLife Readers

©This edition published 2023. First published in 2021.
BookLife Publishing Ltd.
King's Lynn, Norfolk, PE30 4LS, UK

ISBN 978-1-83927-425-1

All rights reserved. Printed in Poland.
A catalogue record for this book is
available from the British Library.

FSC
www.fsc.org
MIX
Paper from responsible sources
FSC® C015559

The Little Painter
Written by Shalini Vallepur
Illustrated by Irene Renon

An Introduction to BookLife Readers...

Our Readers have been specifically created in line with the London Institute of Education's approach to book banding and are phonetically decodable and ordered to support each phase of Letters and Sounds.

Each book has been created to provide the best possible reading and learning experience. Our aim is to share our love of books with children, providing both emerging readers and prolific page-turners with beautiful books that are guaranteed to provoke interest and learning, regardless of ability.

BOOK BAND GRADED using the Institute of Education's approach to levelling.

PHONETICALLY DECODABLE supporting each phase of Letters and Sounds.

EXERCISES AND QUESTIONS to offer reinforcement and to ascertain comprehension.

BEAUTIFULLY ILLUSTRATED to inspire and provoke engagement, providing a variety of styles for the reader to enjoy whilst reading through the series.

AUTHOR INSIGHT: SHALINI VALLEPUR

Passionate about books from a very young age, Shalini Vallepur received the award of Norfolk County Scholar for her outstanding grades. Later on she read English at the University of Leicester, where she stayed to complete her Modern Literature MA. Whilst at university, Shalini volunteered as a Storyteller to help children learn to read, which gave her experience and expertise in the way children pick up and retain information. She used her knowledge and her background and implemented them in the 32 books that she has written for BookLife Publishing. Shalini's writing easily takes us to different worlds, and the serenity and quality of her words are sure to captivate any child who picks up her books.

PHASE 5 /er/ou/

This book focuses on /er/ and /ou/ and the alternative pronunciations of its grapheme. It is a Purple level 8 book band.